DEC. 4/2001

DEAR MARIO

The stories that you
revealed tonight were
quite interesting.
Take care and thank you
for supporting AIDS
research.

People

A Collection of Poetry

Anastasia Fardella

Noble House
Baltimore, Maryland

People
A Collection of Poetry

Library of Congress
Cataloging in Publication Data
ISBN 1-56167-481-8

Library of Congress Card Catalog Number:
98-89645

Published by

8019 Belair Road, Suite 10
Baltimore, Maryland 21236

Manufactured in the United States of America

To my father and mother

CONTENTS

II. ANGST EXCERPTS

III. EXTERNAL VERSES

ACKNOWLEDGEMENTS

I would like to thank Andreas and Penelope Boutas and their family for their support, generosity, and participation in helping me with this book. Zafiris Fardellas, Despina (Daisy) Zaboukos, and Tassos Kapsimalis for their participation and advice. Viv Daskalopoulos for her helpful tips with the camera. John and Vivian Papageorgiou for being themselves, which was both influential and inspirational. I also thank the two individuals who were with me from the very beginning, Chris Kapsimalis and Deborah Hunt. I am forever grateful to my cousin Paul A. Mallos, your assistance and encouragement is greatly appreciated.

INTRODUCTION

People, A Collection of Poetry is a compilation of poems which I have written in the last two to three years. The first poem that I wrote from this collection was "Clandestine."

As I gathered my poems in a folder in 1995, I travelled to Washington D.C. to the International Society of Poets Convention and Symposium to read my poetry. I also wanted to learn more about poetry through fellow poets and lecturers, and to become knowledgeable about the publishing business. Since then, I continued to write about various topics that I felt were important to me and about things that I had experienced in my life or in the lives of people I know. Basically, I wrote these poems from my inner most thoughts and my inspirations.

People, A Collection of Poetry deals with various topics. For instance, "Clandestine" expresses the contradictions of an individual having to deal with personal decisions and trying to compromise those decisions with respect to religion or their deep internal beliefs. "A Poem for Etty" has a different topic as the poem reflects the life of Etty Hillesum, a Jewish lawyer who could have escaped from Nazi persecution, but chose to suffer with her people during the Second World War. Both "Clandestine" and "A Poem for Etty" have a deeper level of meaning which connects these poems. These poems and the entire collection are connected by the theme of struggle. Struggle appeals to a wide audience because of its universality.

Despite the theme of struggle that brings these poems into a collection, *People* has also taken form on another level. I wanted *People, A Collection of Poetry* not to be simply a collection of strong poems hanging together. I wanted one poem to follow the one preceding it in a planned sequence: not too similar but not too disparate.

There are three sections in this book, the first section of poems entitled "It's Me All Right" deals with the individual in society and personal feelings, particularly those dealing with childhood. The second section, "Angst Excerpts" discusses the individual with regard to family and other close personal relationships, and the final section, "External Verses" are poems about the world at large, for example, "Women In War," "Daffodil," "Bread and Roses," etc.

In each section, the poems have been carefully arranged so that they are unique but at the same time they are connected by the topic in a readable organized manner. In "Angst Excerpts," the poem "Pictures" is about family and this is followed by another poem about family, "A Sister, I, and a Brother." Another poem about siblings, "Three Strange Pleasures" follows these poems. The poems that are placed afterwards are about father/child relationships. One such poem "Brass and Sterling" is about a father who has left his country to immigrate to a new land and work very hard to provide for his family. "Kiss Your Father's Feet" is also a poem about a father that has sacrificed his own dreams and goals for his family. These poems are then followed by poems about fathers. For instance, "My Father is King Lear" is about a father's relentless pursuit to build wealth without recognizing the pain his child is suffering, and "Strange Weather" is another poem that discusses a child's ambivalent feelings toward her father. These poems are placed closely together in the same section, page after page. They have topics that are almost similar or they can be linked through the subject, but they are all united by the theme of struggle.

Anastasia Fardella
Montreal, October 1998

IT'S ME ALL RIGHT

THE CHILD INSIDE

Dry sound and image
The rooms are stale.
Instantly,
the couple thought it was love.
Nostalgia rebounds,
it comes around.
The husband says to the
wife, "you are my mother."
The wife responds "you are my father."

THE CAUSE AND EFFECT

His words have fallen
Almost haphazardly
They always fall on me

Belittlement
I am shaken and betrayed
Then he lifts me up

I am brought down
I do not need reverence
I seek approval

I always imagine how
Life will be
I create the memories

I am frightened
In a dark cold room
Ever since I was a child

Outside in the world
Free from a womb
His cold, cold heart

God rescue me.

HER CLOAK

Heaven's Guild
It can get cold
Feeling steel armoured shield

She's abrupt
Her protection is sacred
She refuses to yield

She departs
When there's conversation
You cannot ask questions

She conceals
There's no known fact
There is no known cure

She's angered
With their impassioned curiosity
It's a way to seize her soul

It's a small world
Though it's hard to keep silent
Secrets are a tortured fate

A human virtue
Remains lost in space
Yet no one can really be alone

Many occasions
She hides in disguises
To send tricks of her identity

Her words are bending
Sent in like a desperate hunter
To create a decoy and seek new game

A climate of indulgent gamble
Comparison to the day she lost
Her life was the wager and the cost.

NIGHT

The night
hides my shadow
even the fog
I prevent light
I hate those chandeliers
brightly lit.
In the hallways
of homes,
I want artificial night
To cover the electricity
with sheets.
Night,
the world sleeps
Nothing is clear
for at night
all is still.
From children
in a concentration camp
that cannot whisper after dark.
And an heiress
from the south
making daylight a black cloud.
Night, a convenient shade
as O'Neill's Mary
makes the world go away.

THE TEMPORARY MORGUE

The sun eclipses
But it falls short of breath
By a winter's torment
As I know time finds me.
In these walls,
Hidden from reality.
The castle is crumbling down
Soon the sky opens
With a rain cloud setting in,
The tiger sits still
Then stretches its limbs.

CLANDESTINE

Entrapment has brought me
To seek forgiveness
Among pale contradictions
That God only knows

Body and Soul
I'm alone in my room
Blessed and burdened
With my thoughts torn in two

When I'm in pain
Christ is my drug
As things sacrificed to idols
and I'm left in doubt

Like a thief in the night
I've dodged shadows and
lights, as I have done
Many times before

I am then reborn
but return to desires
Damning my soul
To seek forgiveness

LIKE A SHIP

Sunk like a ship
I reached rock bottom
I had no anchor
Drowning in deep cold water.
I'm the companionship
to the Titanic
Retired like the Blue Nose
left without purpose.
A ship has been replaced
by planes as means
They made me walk the plank
I'm a dying dream.

STORE FRONT WINDOWS

In front of them,
I spent life.
I dazed and they dazzled.
It puzzled me why I thought so hard
Before a fragile world.

I always saw a reflection
Of whom, I was not sure.
The words were lost as I
sought to explain,
what brings me to store front windows again.

GLIMPSE

When the plane touched down
A warm sun welcomed me in the south
Now in the north, as I sit back
A cold winter awaits,
I think back to that time again.
Thwarted by land terrains
And miles of sky,
I retrieve that summer in my mind.

CONFOUNDED

He stood there,
Astute.
With a whip cracked
over his back,
Seizures interrupt peace.
Bright glazed Nazi
Plath knows you
As I know I'm the Jew.
Deep breath exhaled,
no sign of relief
The years have passed
The child always grieves.
Subsist,
Thoughts confiscated
Drowned in the psyche.

SIMILE ME

Flesh.
Hooked up,
a fish from the ocean.
Tonight,
I am someone's dinner.
On the plate,
It's too late,
Saturday night's meal.
I wasn't fond of being
one of those
in the unexplored world.
I am not chattel,
but I remain in reclusion.
I have been caught
too many times
and many days,
I was used for live bait.
I was moist land,
exploited by Cecil Rhodes
I have been colonized,
sold as an export.
I was not a chattel,
but I chose to be.

DILIGENCE

The poison streams are too common
They run in circular motions
Neverending. I took too much trash.
My blood became thick, contaminated
And far too rich for anything good.
I understood that I was meant to last.
Distortion of the mind and senses,
Debilitating. I was lost in perceptions.
I've damaged my body with needles
Then I felt the thorns,
Aftermath. I want to forget the past.
Everybody will fall from grace
Even for a little taste.

A CONSCIENCE

Brandishing knives
And the polish of swords
To fight the bloodiest war.
The hardest fight of all
That may bring regret.

He wants this even
If it makes others upset
He will fight for freedom
The hardest thing yet
To free his mind of turbulence.

And he places upon him
A suit of armour
To lessen his wounds of slaughter.
Avenge of what's been dealt
With an act of hate.

He has chosen the sight
And brings an alibi
His disturbing dreams are going to die
But there will be nowhere
For his conscience to hide.

NORTHERN ESCAPE

I want it to rain on your parade
This motion so deserving
You brought tense moments in this house
I was left to soul searching

The razor cuts deep into the skin
Healed by your palatable words
I climb the walls despairingly
My cries are never heard

Tender touches from your hands
Always try to sink my words
I try to stand on my feet
I wish I had wings like a bird

To go far away from the known
Terrifying things I hold
Escaping to another journey
To migrate from the northern cold

TO VENICE?

Breakfast at noon
Frail bastard,
Why does your heart hurt?
Pain?

They never expect
A soul
to wind down.

Is it because
She is female
Must she slow down?

They pretend
that they need
their daughter.
She's forbidden
to climb a ladder
or travel any distance.

She wants to sing
her own tune
Disregard so-called
Logicians.

Her tongue speaks
showing ground
that remains
alive and well.

Vertigo.
In keeping the light
A blight serene wish
That denies any flight.

The body aches
small pains
Psychosomatic.

In the head
Dreams, secrets
Cross-eyed, blind.

Venice, Italy?
Venice, Florida?
But far from here.

She swears that she
will leave again.

IN REMINISCENCES OF

The sun in winter unfolds
strange opera on the radio.
I think ten years back
again of small images in my mind
and faint conversations.
I watch the highway
in the distance, but it only reminds me
of a similar traffic line
when I fought with my brother.
And today's sun, my first day of college
It seems that I can't leap forward.
Yesterday's long bus ride,
although that is mundane,
only a comparison rises.
Events remain shallow
and the days have drifted by
quickly- Undenied.

THE KEY

In the tiny box-room
There was diffidence
faintly luminous
in depth or in breadth.
Remaining in bitter sleep
with many broken years
exempt from tact.
I feel the goose flesh
while my knees are stiff.

Beauty's carnival
it feels deep, even bittersweet
only indulgence,
and in success,
A traveller needs water
to feed his unrest
A catalyst has the answer
on the television set.

These chains are heavy
Cut this Gordian knot
Even with bloodshed
Devour these sickened thoughts.
So come here Alexander
And take the key
Break all the bonds,
Slay the beast of
possessive greed.

VARIABLE CLOUD STIMULANT

There is not a life on earth
that has seen two days alike
It should not be rendered strange
Under these skies, by design or fate.
The moments of the rain or sun
Under bright clouds, undoubtable praise.
The dark days. Keelhaul, a grey place.
These shoulders are heavy with all that
weight. The barometer, my bones covered
with slate. The caffeine is lost in my
veins as the dispersed intoxicant of rain
brings the stillness of the city.
And the harsh snow breathes depression
on the soil and in my heart,
The dark—where nothing grows.
Exhilaration will soon rise
When the sun starts to shine
I stand tall and walk with my feet
To the horizon, where earth and sky meet.

BURNING LIGHT

Ascension.
I could smell the strong
scent of roses,
Death roses.
Candles are lit
and the smoke rises like ghosts,
stirring souls.
A cognac.
And feel these fingers,
ice cold.
A jellyfish in the ocean,
spoils the gold.
Of all life's wonders,
I have at times felt
the end.
The end of my rope.
Burned.
Moments, they eclipse
When I speak from the
mouths of angels.
Leaning on the gate,
but I cannot stay
The world seems white,
Burning Light.

THE FOREST

Roots, branches, and leaves
A forest's twists and turns
There are seasons with a clearing
Other moments of desolate swamp

Gifted evergreen dance in the wind
White lilac flowers bloom in May
In November it is hard to see through
When mornings are always grey.

If I go through the deep dark forest
Will I find my way back home?
A chance and risk that we take
Where no one could ever know.

There is a tiny green bug on a rock
In the middle of vast hinterland
The flowers bloom, the flowers fade
A spider is caught in the web

A web has twists and turns
Like a maze with many traps
As the spider fights its way
To get back to the top.

In the forest's calm, serene
Up high, there is a sparrow
Hear its magnificent voice sing
Beautiful red, white, and ash wings

At that moment a complimentary white
butterfly stretches and unfolds its wings.

Posed with a pen and paper
Like an artist with a canvas
Painting the forest
With my thoughts and stanzas.

HAILING IN BRAND NEW STRIDE

It's a shame
Of how I wasted all those glorious years
The cause made me grow still

There is sacrilege
When all is evil and remorseful
Captured from the womb to the grave

How we sin?
No one can really be holy
Recommence the majestic feed

The apple of your eye
The core of your heart sees how
I have spent these precious moments

All afternoons
And I had pondered to a faraway place
The longing of my dreams make me wait

The frightening thing
Is that they are so unreal
I will never realize my hopes and dreams

Not all is lost
The utmost moment of happiness reigns
But life will never be the same again

RAGING BUTTERFLY

Its wings like
white linen sheets.
Folding, caressing softly.
It bleeds—if you clip
its wings.
Raging lightly—it will scream.

PROVIDENCE

The wall was built
made new,
Time grew old
It was plastered
through and through.
Transfixed by the beautiful tune,
I rode in divine
put to him by Neptune,
joining his fellow delegates
at the moon.
Marks on the wall
of numbers and names,
Paint has chipped off
the structure remains
of where I've been
or how I came.
If I leave,
the wall remains.

SNOW FIELDS

I struggled to walk through
Bold, courageous in the deep white
Enormous posture and a brave front.
Trudging to make my marks
With some stroke of luck.
But I walk slowly, and I breathe hard
As the wind picks its time to sway me.
In these snow fields, I left prints
and the ice does not aid me.
Those fields are a mask for paradise
when the world is covered in white.

A WINTER'S CROSSING

I remember as young
children
The big field across
my home, covered with snow.
A blanket.
We walked across there,
forming footsteps and setting trails.
Then I moved away and
I hadn't been there for years,
we went back there to reminisce.
But now I lost the imagery of myself
To find the footprints of someone else.

LIFE IN SEPTEMBER

Another year goes by
as my birthday approaches
Every year the same story,
the pulse of life encroaches.
And the stillness of other things
such as falling in love
remain dull, in refrain
from decisions up above.

nothing

I found nothing
all is empty,
inside me.
even a kiss
I can only taste salt
from your tongue.
but no one can
ever understand
the knives
I have received.
I was in a wild state
of killing "beauty."
What is a lie or truth
does not set
our hearts free.
When I was young
You found nothing
inside me
No, you could not
even feel me bleed.
Now, I am older
you say, "you are beautiful"
It is of little concern to me.

ERRAND OF MERCY

A moon's vibrant reflection
on the lake
leaves a sound in my head
I remember it, as I did then.
I sit under the light fixture
to transcend,
something.
Tranquillity.
I thought of those calm waters
I stared at
all the time, in the afternoons
With no one speaking to me
Only a light breeze,
Serenity.
A violent storm clashes madly
caused by rain
The thunder rolls
Designed by me, as I did then.
And comprehend errand of mercy
again.

LETTERHEAD

Edible night,
How can I feast on
these hours?
When I have my tongue
to declare what confines me.
But I never admit the naked truth.
Implicit,
I loathe these heavy stones
That I carry.
The prints I leave with
my walking boots,
or the letterhead left on the desk
for the world to see.

LEXICON

The words I use
Are twisted.
They hurt, by
my own hand
or by someone's plan.
Misunderstood,
with the phrases I use.
Homonyms- similar meanings
or tricks- a Freudian slip.
What's wrong?
But a wretched tongue
emerges the follies of man
And excavates to discover
the real rigor.
And Lexicon rises
like those dug up artifacts
That are misinterpreted
or understood.

WHY SHOULD I SPEAK?

Why should I speak?
I speak, then my words
get twisted.
They are turned into
your juxtaposition.
Why should I speak?
You have already tainted
my phrases,
Presenting a novelty but
tormenting my senses.
Why should I speak?
When you revise my feelings
and views,
Creating your tales or
fables, your truth.
Why should I speak?
I'm alone in my solitude
In my own confine
I speak my own mind.

WORDS

The ink has dried out
The paper is brittle and rough
It's hard to write on
My words are distraught.

Incapable of any touch
Alone, abandoned in a room
To heal my wounds
And betray the truth

except for this paper,
to reveal my words....

LINES

It's a race,
I am upset,
Time keeps running,
I'm just building thoughts.
Through hard terrain,
I am struggling
To produce lines
And fill this page.

THIS PAGE

Time sounds vast
But it deeply changes
When in moments you are
sound asleep.

When happiness reigns
As you are well liked
The future seems glorious
While the benefits reap.

Conviction settles
Questions in lingering doubt
With the days getting darker
Whilst your fruits shrivel and rot.

Youth is always sweet
It lingers slowly like
Soft honey from a tree.

Eventually you will age
Without having worked
Or really earned your wage.
What will be made of you?
Nothing; but this page.

MANY SUMMERS AGO

Many summers ago
I was a young child in the
process of learning.
Struggle and persistence
To become one of whole.

Many summers ago
I had many fields to cross but
I passed and fell behind.
Ambition and failure
A combination of nature.

Many summers ago
I held out for myself to assist
deviant and disobedient peers.
Envy makes one hungry
Leaves the soul empty.

Many summers ago
I began searching for something
to call my own.
My thoughts preoccupied me
Entering fear of the unknown.

Many summers ago
I could not remember any
dreams and memories.
Alterations that time brings
Yet I was here many summers ago.

ANGST EXCERPTS

ALONE

With the moon I see a shadow
It even passes me by in daylight
I feel frightened and it's late
The precious whisky just can't wait
Alone in the inn followed by hope
But I remain without a partner.

Follow others to their space
But they all have lovers.
There are times when I feel it's best,
Yet I need someone.
At the pond, by the bridge
I look for one who looks for me
I see a shadow by the moon,
but it passes me
It passes me.

VINCENT'S EAR TO A PROSTITUTE

I never saw alone,
someone more alone than me
Could that be the reason
why he painted beautifully
of those Dutch lands
and the peasants in the fields.
The stroke of a brush
on a starry, starry night
and even a tune from Don McLean
to honour this man's life.
His thoughts in colours
that make circles in patterns.
Vincent became confused,
because he never found a friend
only to live for his art
until the very end.

SIBERIAN SUMMER

As I stared
into the open arms of the sun,
I searched for warmth
but it was so cold.
I thought I would hear
a soft voice
Only to receive a winter's scold
again,
every year.

FRAYED AFFAIRS

Xtra stems of long roses
in your bedroom
Can you open your eyes?

Many times he says
"I love you"
That's what you want?

You know how many times
men said that to me?
It is only words

There are golden moments
But you must find them
on your own

No man can provide
life, only some shared dreams
and hopes

Expectations are wrong,
they falter and they break
Many times he says
"I love you"
this causes a heart to ache.

UNSPOKEN

Solid fabric
Interwoven
Placed in detergent
Pulled apart from the seams
Slowly unfolding.
Falling apart
From day to dusk
Receiving a fair warning
As a thread departs another
So does my love for you
Unspoken.

FORCING LOVE

Fate needs to be sealed
and some decide to change things
For better or worse,
but they decide.

Love is not wise
Nor a calculated fact,
It's not math.

A Canadian songwriter
once said, "Don't look, you won't find it."
Crossing the border
Once more, again.
Betwixt and between
Still? And Yet? Deliberate.
Thoughts oscillate.

They believe they will live
forever, searching for love
Insisting they will not fail.

LIFE'S TRAGICOMEDY

My cousin is a poet
an apparition like a dream
holds confetti in his hands
Love is blind, love is king

She holds terror
And her rules reign
A love affair
Immersed in pain

He convinces me that
He holds the key
He has laughter while
She yanks his neck

If we perish in life
Then we perish in death
When do our lives really end?

There are destinies in compass
Only bicycles with spokes
Deserting charity and caring
Leaves us lying in the cold

DISLOYAL

I've read all of your poems
Throughout the entire night
To wake up to a dusk grey morning
Stone hedges falling off buildings
Waterways are flooding,
Many cataclysmic warnings.

There are many hopes to hold on to
But there are those that let go
They stop chasing the rainbows
or the wishes of spirits
On their many occasions
Inviting irony and rages.

She remains innocent and true to thee
Although you've always been
Chosen from an evil beauty
Sacrificing all souls leaving nobody,
I want to prevent Holy Matrimony

Gospels sung in his memory
Black cars roll past the hills
You are an angel now
Have you earned your wings?
You are an angel now
Have you earned your wings?

AN APARTMENT IN D.C.

The silver chair, there
in the corner.
I feel this room
present with despair.

In afternoon,
With a sun brightly lit
But it does not seep
Through indolence.

The thick plastic table
Those long black Bauhaus beds
the cages in the kitchen
where the plumage rests

Squalid nest.

Walls and high ceilings
Neutral, left nondescript
Three hundred and sixty degrees
of bitterness.

Everywhere, glass objects
with sharp piety
encased in a menagerie.

I heard a harsh melody
In these halls
It terrifies me.

At the top, the last
floor.
Inside those heavy
dark doors.
Is this what a dream reveals?

MEN LEAVE

Washing laundry
All her life
To get the clothes cleaned
Because before Sunday,
She has four mouths to feed
in an urban ghetto,
in a lousy dream.
When there are families
but the men leave.
This boy
Knows no father
He will walk in life incomplete
not bound by honour
Living on the cold streets
in an urban ghetto,
in a lousy dream.
The boy is now man
With several mouths to feed
but he will run like his father
because men leave.

BOOMERANG

the strides of courage rising
but the Gestapo
makes its mark,
again—on her heart.
upholds tenets
Rhetoric.

the bleeding stops
when the blitzkrieg subsides
Momentarily.
But it comes back again
as does the tide to the shore
Once more.

a black and blue reflection
in the mirror
Is a window open?
She feels cold,
even if he slams the door.

she wants to swim
against the waves of war
this wife will be back, once more
in the hope of a better man
to the shore.

TO LOVE A PASSPORT

A passport
Cannot talk back.
It is a friend,
A Companion.
It takes you everywhere.

For freedom, wealth
even imagination, success.
Access.
A land to uncover
and undress your dreams,
Long pink dress.

There is a passport;
The body of a red car
in her dream,
She thought of him.
Their partnership
fled to another continent
And so it attracts him,
the land of capitalism.
To marry a passage.

She is a passport,
a ship to a port.
The amount of lost words between
a burning desire for change.
He tries to love her.

He left her land
to go south for warmth.
He cannot love.
He left her north
in the cold
She stands alone.

TROJAN'S GAME

A noble act in asking
of love's resolute,
And in the confines
of these walls,
Pax Romana.
I opened up the devil's
room,
swindled by the sultans
They welcomed me with dances
and fruits.
I remember from those
sophists,
that great big war
Where they built
a wooden horse
I watch closely
that chess board.
For a manoeuvre or
any sign of life
But the stare of
a Cheshire cat
Hides the darkness
of your mind.
And if Paris loved
greatly, then he was
a fool
The kind of love that
is too deep,
blinding and cruel.
I ponder meticulously
to make a move
I hear those careful
whispers and soft lies

to cajole my intentions
and let down my guard.
Since those past centuries
of what they've known
this world is divided
between love and war.
Currently, brave soldiers
will dress tonight in uniform
to checkmate a heart
on a black and white board.

IN SALOME'S GARDEN

Insulated to protect my feet
from getting wet,
and these are strange woods
of clever craft and intent.
There are leaks
when something sneaks
or crawls in,
and slithers smoothly
under your skin.
In Salome's garden,
From the first taste
of medicine—
bitter on my tongue,
poisoned from her dancing.
Under the sky,
left on the plate
to bleed to death,
in Salome's garden
of clever craft and intent.

WHEN VENGEANCE SLEEPS

When Vengeance sleeps
I will be in peace
And far away from here
As love begets hate
From one source or another
I shall know for I
am awake.

When Vengeance speaks
And I drift in silence
To turn my back to reality
It will hurt me- like
it has done for others
But there is no vengeance
inside me.

When Vengeance sleeps
I will lie awake to
wait for its resurface
I shall know its form,
its bitter taste
Under the volcano
it is always awake.

HOUSE PROWLER

A bug crept slowly
Inch by inch
Trying hard not to
disturb the peace.
Searching for food,
House prowler!
Through the cracks
Into the cupboards.
To feed oneself
Digesting curious intent
Dropping the crumbs
On a canopy bed.

THE SPIDER AND THE FLY

He invites me into the parlour
Like the spider and the fly
To dissect the daily bread
Missing from his own life.
"Laugh a little," my mother tells me
"It's much worse to be gripe
If you are angry or upset
He will deem your soul, his right."
And by the window pane there sits,
the little fly inside
sitting far from the spider
that tries to take another bite.

REVERSAL OF FORTUNE

I am a villain
A traitor, a thief
I robbed your caverns
When you were asleep.

I relished in silence
When you lost your wealth
And flew like an eagle
With wings of stealth.

And to everything
There is a beginning and end
And a tragedy has its turn
of what is heaven's send

And now I suffer
with bitter pills to swallow
Losing all of prosperity
Even hiding from my own shadow.

THE ROAD OF COBBLESTONES

Charlatans surround me,
they claim imagination
to arouse admiration
influence or peddle
an idea, or perhaps a scheme.
But as of late,
they tried to delight
and some whistle
lightly like the dealers
at a horse track.
They feed me accolades
but they plot behind my back
They please you in the aftermath,
after all that.
Everyone walks in their own shoes,
from the wide open spaces
of the world.
Signs of directions;
distances, limits, and curves.
I continue clumsily, inept
but remain ill-humoured.
There is no "friend"
all the lines on my hands,
the rejection I sometimes felt.
Ruffians kneel before me
for my love to be imminent.
My peers all swagger
on the road of cobblestones
but I have walked
on my own.

THE NAME WITHHELD

Thoughts stored inside
Ideas left unexplained
Kept, for the self
To hold and protect.

Bereaved, inside a hole
It could be in the head
or in a desk?
Stored behind a door,
On a shelf? Who knows?

Wires speak, lead
to a closed circuit.
A smile, the wisest guise
Digress from diplomacy
but the heckles rise.

The use of elements
even incense
Does not make enemies forget
The things you hold dear,
the name withheld.

ABSURD

Pebbles and stones
under the white snow
or on a beach.
Immediately, camouflaged
strokes.

The grave marking
from the sun
the water is full of salt
And no one knows
how the ties bind.

Tonight, a victim
The next day, a bitter taste
Betrayal at our feet
But it's absolved, wasted away.

She stands, a lay figure
Lawless, her face of marble
with bare hands we work.
Absurd. Absurd.

You can call her Judas
Stealing-traitor
Absurd.
And her stare like winter
Sitting amongst us
at the dinner.

The eyes, portent
False gratitude
she plays the strings of a lyre
Dirges are heard.

letters on parchment
I would leave,
but I can't, my flesh and blood?
To tear the bond from
the one that loves
Yet these are just words,
Absurd. Absurd.

BUTTONS ON A SHIRT

Buttons on a shirt
Comfortably sewn
Five buttons on their own
Interrelated like a family at home
Complete.

Buttons on a shirt
Tightly held by thread
As are people to family ties
The pattern is what binds
Togetherness.

Buttons on a shirt
Threatening! A thread is loose
A button is breaking free
It has fallen off,
Tragically!

THE PICTURES

The merchandise fell to the floor,
or left speechless on the furniture
Long regretting memories that
flood back like the tide.
Along the beach house where we stayed
Reflecting freeze-framed memories
Capturing days of youth.
Unspoken, having a story of their own
Pictures; companions when I'm alone.

INSISTENT SONNET

Perish—you do not deserve life
Because you take the life out of me
Others say it's selfish and unfair
Causing great despair in a family

Reviving our spirits to destroy them again
So I have planned her long epitaph
With a mother's plea and intrusion
Determined that she pays this wrath

Although I may be invective
She has robbed our sacred possessions
Her hands held tightly around the swords
She has caused the family segregation

There are others extremely resistant
but I am angered and insistent.

A SISTER, I, AND A BROTHER

I'm in the middle of both of you
Never knowing who I am
You both tore me in two
Shattering my persona in half.

Abstinence may be cruel
When it plans to define you
You stand divided like a wall
Never knowing who's side you're on.

I'm tired of being a go-between
Like a neutral Switzerland
Standing on guard as a troubleshooter
Amongst a sister and a brotherland.

And to remain there compassionate
To merely accommodate the rising war
Restricted to reason with you
Propagating me as your clone

THREE STRANGE PLEASURES

We came in threes, didn't we?
At different times, of the same womb.
An order in a mother's universe.

In recent waves of small operators
a density of another kind
measures of the first born
undisputed star, rises above
the impact on the vast crowds
the big bang, cosmic supernova.
Even in cyberspace, she can push you over.

We shall dance in three
I am always placed in-between
Limbo finds the chords for a melody.
Travelled by thoughts, a dance in pairs
one shall be left to dance with herself.
I see blood red, the waves above my head,
electromagnetic or kinetic.
Stretched out in full view,
my patience learned of elasticity
I lean on one foot; balanced
to alleviate the other.
A trapeze act, on the high wire.

And last, saved for the hugely famous
who plays the fiddle well
recognition stems from praise
small sly manoeuvres for discursiveness.
Forthright critical protection
does not create an atmosphere of scars
Only the intimately assured benefits
for the child most truly loved.

How strange, we three?
An odd number featured...

THE YEARS OF DISPARITY

WHY couldn't you learn to
speak the language
in a country with a modern tongue?
It would be easier to understand,
instead of asking me.
And I seem daft to everyone.
WHY don't you drive?
The only thing you do
is stir the incompassion
in me, sometimes.
I wish you knew something
to release me.
But there is space,
incongruence running
through the years
between a mother and daughter,
disparate dreams.
WHY couldn't you marry
much earlier than thirty-eight?
It took that long to feel settled?
Instead, you gave birth later.
And I know your charms in life
that you came far from here,
were nothing but an ordeal.
WHY do I waste time
to regurgitate what has been done?
But to allow the distance to carry on.

A PORCELAIN VASE

There is a dark room,
where she breathes alive with sound
her heart has sunk, self confined.
In the care of servants with white coats,
Slowly life fades. Love begins with the
porcelain vase.

It is merely an object,
perhaps nothing more in the corner,
a sullen green of Grecian design.
Strategically placed on a dresser
in a room that is dark as night.

Nothing of marquetry
or the like of crown jewels
There is no deep sentiment,
only the need to display it.

Carefully, she wraps a royal purple cloth
And she runs in now and then -
before her guests to wipe off the dust.

And the flesh upon flesh
slowly melts, the crimson residue remains.
Decomposition is just the same.

Where do the ashes of her mother rest?
Inside the dark room, in a porcelain vase.

BRASS AND STERLING

He brought over souvenirs
Of memories past

They were not
Brass and Sterling
Materials meant to last

His tired heavy hands
Have worked for miles
In a strange land
He came without language

What's more, he's the hardest
Working man I know.

Hesitant registration
The guilt I undergo
I am born here
A fault I know

Steel cold nights
Lonely streets
Only in dark shadows
Marked beyond retreat

Grappling far from over
Columbus at his feet
My father suffered greatly
But he never faced defeat.

KISS YOUR FATHER'S FEET

Honour him,
It's the First Commandment
of God.
Wash his feet, as she
did for Jesus.

There is only one,
He can't truly be replaced
Remember the parable of
the Prodigal Son?

This is not for all fathers,
Only mine
Shedding his life to prevent
my demise.

He suffered greatly
Bearing his own cross
With his tired heavy feet
and his lungs breathing hard.

If he has lived his life harshly,
you must beseech.
Honour him,
Kiss your Father's feet.

MY FATHER IS KING LEAR

Come, speak to me
I've waited all these years
for you to let me be
And to tell me how you feel.

Conspiracy has gathered
Suspicion has made him austere
With three dancing daughters
My father is King Lear.

The castle changes hands
With time, a loss of power
Reagan and Goneril's avarice
To climb the castle's tower.

My father will hand his crown
But he stands hammer and sparrow
His children await in ceremony
but he does not see the sorrow.

A kingdom built with prizes
Why did you bore me slave/master?
I don't live for the wealth
I am innocence, the third daughter.

There are those words of hurt
When a daughter bleeds under duress
The lawyers plan a tapestry
Weaving phrases with finesse

I stand amongst these shadows
In reprieval and fear
What has become of us?
My father is King Lear.

And now my dear father,
You see me after all these years
I will die like Cordelia
But you have lived like Lear.

FOUR-FIFTY

The weather outside
Brought me to a day
so familiar.
The obstacle beside
me, all day in a bed
marked with pain.

And I chose to speak
again, a reminder of
what is real.
Don't be afraid and say
"You'll never see me"
I too, will die someday.
Now, I forget the details
But it was Four-Fifty,
Time to set the clock again.

A FUTURE ELEGY, BUT WHO KNOWS WHEN?

I look up to the sky
Prolonging the inevitable.
I've seen pools of blood,
A crime,
If those lights are shut off.
The knives - cigarettes and drinks
We are balancing on high wires.
Save my father from eternity,
the one that goes beyond me.
I don't want forever sleep.

STRANGE WEATHER

A child
Guilt ridden
And other times sure.
A replica of a father
but it falls short.

There is a warm
sun that he provides
In these comfort rooms
where neglect dies.

A pleonastic provider
work possesses him
spending on properties
to improve and maintain them.
Working harder than ever before
for Uncle Sam or the tax man.
I feel at fault.

Reality is at the door,
Consumption.
I can see his red skin
Swollen belly from the drinks.

I know you've raised
me from a seed
But you made
the weather change,
those waves pull me in.

I am under
Here in these words
I elucidate the chit-chat.

A comment,
a name that made
me feel so small.

Hidden from the frozen rain
Underneath a shell
It felt cold around me
from the inside of a room.

I hover like the seal
that's about to be clubbed.
Wide eyes, innocent.
Meek.

I sit alone, stiff
falling on my face.
When do we wrong?
Dark,
without electric light.
A touch,
Ice. Ice.
A father's
WELCOME mat.

GROWING APART

The trails taken
Walked or breathed
It hadn't stopped
those dandelions from growing.
Then I made trails
apart from your path
Parallel to the
train tracks.
To race with speed,
Growing apart.

EXTERNAL VERSES

VICISSITUDE SPEAKS

Vicissitude speaks
A tongue unknown
When a lover slams the door.

Complications arise
With a different pace
As provisions fall to the floor.

Carnations bloom
A season has passed
Nothing remains the same anymore.

DAFFODIL

Pale and vagrant lives
Turbulent and doleful times
Shattering a distance between two points
Swelling engagements at the joints

I place my faith in daffodil
Revealing things I never will
Determined with no one to know
The daffodil can only grow

It will grow strong and still
Precious companionship of my daffodil
Treasuring it most intense
It is the daffodil that I love best

Sharing thoughts in diffusive face
Crossing boundaries for an embrace
A simple love that makes me feel
The comfort of the daffodil

Trudging through open fields
Welcoming strangers for their peace
Peerage has produced the pain
Alone in the fields again

I run in fields but seasons passed
The daffodils could not last
The machines levelled the fields
A tempestuous nature had them cleared.

BREAD AND ROSES

Many humans, few jobs
A tragedy of the twentieth century
The marching women in Quebec
Bread and roses to have the children fed

Estimates, projected and rejected
A summary of what women were taught
To be good mothers and wives
Rising costs: they were caught

Women with babies
Must have them to care
They must struggle to work
They pull more than their share

I work hard and I pray to God
Save me from this trail
Help me from marching
I do not want to fail

In high contract walls
The set up of fancy schemes
Has shed all the working world
It has done me in

A HUNGRY WORLD

Blood stains on his shirt
His wrists slashed
He's not hurt.
There is a need to fight back
That's when he feels alone
Their lives are not the same any more
In a cold hungry world.

DENSE INTENSITY

What rekindled anger,
A wayward hand?
The lost desire of
a nowhere man.
He wears a black
rim hat
A dark overcoat
He wanders aimlessly
Throughout the corridors.
A gun in a case
A mind in overdrive
He pulls the trigger
For his anger to die.

VICTIMS

It was a ray of light in my coffee,
I threw out the paper cup.
A delicate matter,
Nothing more.
A fly lying at my door.
Does a man kill a woman,
out of love or hate?
Does he bite his nails
to kill the taste?
That night I wept slowly
To see the world sin.
There was no remorse
when the world fell in.

ABOUT A DEAD WINTER

The armies went south
When the rain came down hard
In this shanty town,
In this lousy dream.

During the summer,
You can hear their feet
Hitting the pavement
In the dry heat.

When they are here,
It's pure madness
But I would rather have that
Than silence.

WORLD DECEASED

Fallacy brings remorse
When a hero closes the door

Anger renders into despair
When others do not take time to care

Isolation withers companionship
When one chooses to be alone

Secrets are in all doors
And you store the key to your heart

A lack of connection stales
The vagrancy leaves generations pale.

THE LAST DECADE

Skinned animals for
their precious pelts
To buy and sell.

A marriage dowry
to give and take
Involving exchange.

Letting the tigers loose
from their cage,
Watching the birds
fight over the bread.

THE EYE OF A HUNTER

Grazed skin
Deep within the woods.
Skylark ocean
dancing victorious.
Exploring, the wind
keeps blowing.

RED RIVER

The river,
it floods
red streams, pulsing hard
pushing through mud and rocks.
Injected by a demagogue.
The river runs to smaller veins
flowing violently in its course
to the arms of the sea,
weapons of war; guns and greed.
This red river
cannot be held by a dam
a schism in a sandbag,
and it overflows beyond the banks.

POEM FOR ETTY

Dedicated to the memory of Etty Hillesum who died at Auschwitz, a Nazi concentration camp.

Etty it's brave
You chose to suffer
When you could have escaped
Etty it's praise

Your life full of promise
But you chose to suffer
With high accomplishments
Etty it's honourable

Sent to Auschwitz
You left singing
And God understands
Etty it's pride

I hold your letter
With a dear embrace
Tears from my eyes
Etty it's grace

You saw the devil
Yet you held strong
You left us a letter
And even a song

The violins wail
The trains rolling out
Goodbye Etty,
Victim of the Holocaust.

WOMEN IN WAR

A disaster bug
Becomes hard hit
War has come.
National pride rides
Supposed ethnic cleansing
Heartless men!
Women do not fight
They pay the biggest price
Humiliation to produce.
I close my eyes
Heartless veins!
Men carried off and killed
Women and children in the streets.
Rape, the cruelest deed.
Babies born unloved
Mothers don't want them
Forced upon them.
Soldiers? Heartless beasts!
Placing women in humility
But it's their shame
Their sour veins.
Women in war
Like those in my family
Have suffered greatly.

ANOTHER NUMBER

He showed me the
number marked on his arm
It can't come off.

He was born in Salonika
a long time ago
but he's never been back.

He's not famous or rich
just a man on the street.
He is not one for fame or glory,
only retreat.

And he spoke Greek
to me,
those words.
Words I never heard.

He bears many scars
I can't see.
Not just the symbol
on his arm that he showed me.

He has a name
but I don't know it yet.
He is not simply
a number left on a desk.

MEN

Their meticulous nature,
so strange.
Screaming,
Then to be sweet again.
Enraged.
Men,
their desires and
hates.
Deliberate intent—
that's why they run countries
With fierce descent
And that's why they start wars
that we can't comprehend.

THE WHITE DOVE

It was morning
As I lay down
under the sun.
I saw a dove up above,
flying in circles,
caressing the sky.
I was pleased
to wear a wreath
of olive leaves,
when the afternoon
came - and the walls
were torn down.
They started slowly
when they began to speak.
At last, we can breathe
From detente to rapprochement:
We now have peace.

A DAY ON EARTH

The monarch crawls on the rose bush,
chews on the leaves. There are nothing
but holes. The green colour will fade,
and the yellow-black ugly skin swarms
up the stems. Nature blends, to take
its course. Through metamorphosis
to open the doors.
A peaceful state.

BLACKENING

In a white space
unmarked, things get dark-
and if you add a little gray
it gets lighter by the shade.
It is either black or white
It is wrong or it is right
It is day or it is night.
The keys on a piano
A flounder, on each side a
different colour.
The stripes of the zebra,
a dalmatian,
and so many other things.
Old TV and photographs
white flowers, black clouds.
BLACKENING.
dark, thick as fog and
dense.
See all the people run,
they are gone,
EXODUS.
empty   spaces
in   be   tween.
And what do you suppose
all these phrases mean?